Stephen – Learning about Meningitis

Stephen – Learning about Meningitis

Jenny Wilson

Christian Focus

ISBN 1 85792 572 6

©Jenny Wilson

Published in 2000
by
Christian Focus Publications
Geanies House, Fearn,
Ross-shire, IV20 1TW, Great Britain

Cover design by Owen Daily

With my thanks to
all the friends
who prayed for us

1

'Hush my baba! Go to sleep,' I whispered to my whimpering eight week old son Stephen, as he lay restlessly in his cot. 'Shhh! calm down, my pet. Close your pretty wee eyes.'

I stroked his hair. I patted his back. I tried to cut myself off from his constant whimpering. If only he would go to sleep! All he needed was a good sleep. Stephen had been in one of those feeding and semi-sleeping moods all day: starting to feed, falling asleep, then waking up just minutes later crying for more. He wasn't getting enough milk to satisfy him or enough sleep to keep him happy. The women at church had taken it in turns to rock him, all hoping that they still had the knack from their own child rearing days. But as soon as he drifted off and a triumphant look crossed a woman's face, Stephen's screaming had started again.

'It's probably the curry that I ate last night,' I had said to them, trying desperately to think of some excuse for my son's distress. Now, several hours later, it was not much better. If only he would go to sleep!

'Let me take him for a while,' Alistair said. 'You go and make yourself a coffee.'

Leaving my husband to soothe his tiny son, I went downstairs to the sitting room. The girls were fighting over a piece of paper.

'Stop it, girls. Don't make a noise, you'll wake up Stephen,' I cried.

'He's already awake,' Rachel shouted back at me. 'So it doesn't matter how much noise we make.'

I lifted my hand, ready to smack the cheeky, impudent four year old who stood so defiantly in front of me.

'How dare you speak to me like that,' I shouted, bringing my hand down on her leg.

For a moment after that slap there was total silence.

'That was sore! You're a naughty, naughty Mummy.'

I ran sobbing to the kitchen. Throwing myself to the floor I cried, 'Lord, I'm not coping. You've got to do something to help me! I can't go on! Help me. Please!'

Frightened by my unusual outburst, the children sat subdued and confused on the settee.

Alistair came down the stairs with Stephen still screaming in his arms. I knew from his face that he too was confused. Who needed his help most? His sobbing wife? His crying baby? His two troublesome girls? There's a limit to what a man can do!

No matter how much we cuddled him, Stephen continued to scream.

'I think the wee soul's in pain,' Alistair suggested. 'Maybe we should call the doctor.'

'It's probably just wind,' I said through my subsiding tears. 'Or he could be picking up on my stress. I don't want to bother the doctor on a Sunday evening unless it's really urgent. It could even be an ear infection. They probably wouldn't give him anything anyway. Give him to me and you go and pack so you are ready to go in the morning.'

I laid Stephen down in his reclining chair. There was so much to do! I had a whole list of things: iron shirts even though it was Sunday, wash the dishes, put out school clothes for morning, prepare a packed lunch for Alistair to have on his trip to Wales, feed the children and put them to bed then make several phone calls. But Stephen needed me. The girls needed me. And I needed sleep!

As Stephen lay whimpering, his eyelids began to close. He was asleep at last. I could feel the tension in me subsiding. Then, with a violent jerk, his arms and legs flew outwards, his eyes opened and he started screaming again. With a sinking heart I picked him up. His screaming grew worse. Lost for anything else to do, I put him back down in his cot. Stephen lay whimpering, his tiny eyelids struggling to close as he fell asleep only to be jerked awake again, screaming in pain and protest. I tried to feed him, but he didn't even want to latch on. I still had not done the ironing. Alistair needed those shirts to take away with him.

'I'll do them later if I get a chance,' Alistair said. 'If not, I'm sure there will be ironing facilities in Wales.'

Leaving my distressed baby uncomforted, I made tea for the girls while Alistair went out to church. He had to. He was preaching! My head thumped. The girls played up. And Stephen still either screamed or whimpered. When Alistair came home he put the girls to bed. I was so worn out I went to bed with Stephen.

'Maybe if I feed him lying down, he'll fall asleep,' I hoped aloud to Alistair. It did seem to be better. As long as Stephen was lying, he seemed to flit in and out of sleep. Although he wouldn't feed, his screaming subsided at last. All night long he whimpered and slept, whimpered and slept.

And it was a very long night. I was so tired but I couldn't let sleep overcome my exhaustion. I prayed and prayed, constantly looking at my watch. Slowly, ever so slowly, the minutes and hours ticked by. Time always seems to go at its slowest through the dark night hours. Reassured by Stephen's relative peace I felt sure that, with a new day, everything would be all right again. Children go up and down so quickly.

I remembered calling out a doctor on a Sunday evening for Bethany when she, not much older than Stephen, had behaved in a very similar fashion. After a long wait the doctor had appeared, examined her briefly, then advised us to give her paracetamol. 'It's probably just a virus,' we were told. 'Children tend to pick them up. She'll probably be back to normal tomorrow.' And he was right. By the next day she was as happy as ever, with no signs of the previous evening's upset. I had felt so guilty at calling him out for such a trivial thing that I was determined not to do the same again. But, despite that, there was a slight warning niggle at the back of my mind.

'Lord, help us,' I prayed. 'Keep my children safe. How I wish Alistair wasn't going away tomorrow. Please can you stop him?' I wanted so much to ask him to stay at home but I knew I couldn't. And, after all, this was probably just one of those minor childhood ailments that flare up suddenly and then die down just as quickly. Tomorrow Stephen would be better and his daddy's staying behind would have been pointless.

Alistair's working trip to Wales was of considerable importance. He had just started a new job as New Testament Lecturer with the Highland Theological Institute in Elgin. As the degree they were offering to students was validated by the University of Glamorgan for the course's first few years all the teaching staff were required to attend planning meetings in Wales. To stay at home because one of the family members was a bit off colour was to our minds not an option.

The night wore on. I desperately wanted to phone the doctor, but kept thinking of that poster in his surgery. 'A tired doctor is a bad doctor. Think twice before you call him out in the night.'

'They are right,' I thought. 'Things are always different in the daylight.'

At the back of my mind I was worried, not only about Stephen, but also about how I would cope while Alistair was away if I didn't get enough sleep. I knew that without sleep I was inclined to be grumpy with the children. And I had no-one I felt I could ask to look after the children for an hour or so to let me have forty winks. Feeling as though Alistair's return was several years away rather than just a few days, I went to God for help. 'Lord please give me some sleep,' I pleaded. 'I am your beloved,' I cried. 'You promised in your word to give your beloved sleep. Please Father, give us both some sleep!'

I must have drifted in and out of sleep, but in the night it is hard to keep any sense of time. The dark hours did pass and, as I watched my fretful son, I also watched the light of the rising sun flickering through the curtains.

Ironing

There is so much to do today!
Bags to pack, and children to wake.
Prayers to say,
And breakfast to make.
But Stephen is crying,
And I still haven't ironed the shirts!

There is so much to do today!
The kids to bath, the lunch to make.
The floor to hoover,
The grass to rake.
But Stephen is crying,
And I still haven't ironed the shirts!

There is so much to do today!
The kids to dress, the downies to shake.
The dishes to wash,
And cakes to bake.
But Stephen is crying,
And I still haven't ironed the shirts!

There is so much to do today!
But now it's too late, it will all have to wait.
Life is more precious
Than housework and bakes.
Stephen's stopped crying
And I can't care less about the shirts!

2

I was awake when the alarm rang at 5:30 the next morning. Alistair busied himself, getting ready to join the rest of the staff who were travelling with him on the ten hour journey to Wales.

'Did Stephen sleep at all?' Alistair asked. He had slept in the spare bedroom as he was to be taking his share of the driving.

'A bit,' I replied. 'On and off. I think that I'll phone the doctor as soon as the surgery opens. He's still got a very high temperature. He probably has an ear infection. I don't want to give him Calpol. It says on the bottle that it is only for children over three months and he's just eight weeks. I'll ask the doctor.'

'Do you want me to stay?' Alistair asked.

'No, we'll be fine,' I answered. 'Once he gets some antibiotics he'll soon pick up.'

'I could stay and take the train down later,' he suggested.

'No. You need to go. We'll be fine,' I said, again trying to convince myself as much as him, although I did feel more positive now. Daylight had made everything feel better.

A horn beeped outside. Alistair looked out the window at the wakening morning.

'That's the mini bus,' he said. 'I must go. I'll phone when we arrive tonight and hear how you get on at the doctor.' A quick kiss and a cuddle, a slight hesitation and he was gone. Suddenly fear set in again. It is amazing how lonely you can feel when you are frightened. I wanted to scream out, 'Don't go! Stay! I need you!' But my constant inbuilt feelings of duty kept my mouth shut. Like many other women I felt, quite wrongly, that my needs always had to come last.

Rachel got herself dressed, and I dressed two year old Bethany.

'Will I cuddle Stephen, Mummy?' asked Rachel. 'Then you could get the breakfast in peace.' Looking down at my precious girl, who had so nearly come to harm at my hands the previous night, I wanted to scoop her up in my arms and plead for forgiveness. 'I'm sorry that I was so grumpy yesterday darling,' I said, bending over and kissing her.

'It's all right Mummy,' she said. 'I do love you.'

'Thanks, darling,' I smiled, laying her little brother on her knee. 'I'm sure Stephen could do with a cuddle just now. I don't think that he is very well.'

To the sound of Stephen's whimpering I made the children their breakfast. Suddenly I realised there was silence. I ran through. Rachel sat as stiff as a board with tears sparkling in her eyes. Stephen lay peacefully in her arms.

'Is he dead, Mum?' she asked in a frightened little voice.

I went over and looked at the little face snuggled up against his sister's shoulder. I felt his head.

'No darling,' I assured her. 'Feel how hot his head is. Look at his chest moving up and down. That's him breathing. Stephen is alive but he's not very well. You've helped him to sleep when Mummy couldn't do it. Stephen must think you are a very special big sister.'

So as not to disturb Stephen, I fed Rachel while she cradled her precious little brother.

When I phoned the surgery the receptionist told me that I could see a doctor at 10 o'clock. That gave me time to take Rachel to school.

My next door neighbour arrived with her granddaughter. This had become a daily occurrence since Rachel started school the previous week. Iris nursed Stephen, while I got the girls' coats on. My friend looked tired. She was undergoing chemotherapy, having had a mastectomy. The week before we moved into the house Iris found a lump on her breast, and

17

the next day was admitted to hospital where cancer was diagnosed. We grew very close during her illness. How I would have got through Stephen's illness without Iris, I don't know. I am so grateful for the provision God made of people to help and support us in those weeks.

As we waited for the school bell to ring Stephen started his screaming again. I rocked the pram and shoogled it. I talked soothingly to him and stroked his head. Nothing I did calmed him, and I felt my face reddening under the cold gazes of my fellow parents. I was new to the area and, apart from Iris, I knew no-one. I stood there as the stranger with the screaming child.

The bell rang, and I watched my fearful four year old walking slowly into school lagging behind the rest of her class. Looking miserable, she turned to me with a frightened, trapped look. She hadn't taken to school yet. I knew she wanted me to go into her classroom with her for a short time. But not today. I couldn't. There was so much to do. Rachel had had such a lot to cope with in her little life. My pregnancy with Stephen had not been easy, and I had been on crutches for a large part of it. We hadn't managed to do all the exciting things we normally did. Even walks in the park were difficult, and any outing had to be planned around whether there were stairs for me to negotiate. When our son was only days old we moved to Elgin and Rachel started school a few weeks later, knowing no-one. She desperately missed her friends in Inverness and longed to go back. Just a few days before Stephen took ill she had a phone call from the head teacher at her old nursery school in Inverness, asking how she had settled into school. After the call Rachel sat down on the living room floor crying. 'I hate Elgin. I hate my new school. I hate my new house.' And I had to agree with her. I hated it too. It had been a tough time for all of us and now, as life seemed to be settling down into some sort of routine, the pace and stress was beginning to show.

I remember reading a book that listed the top ten stresses we can face. Moving house, changing job and having a baby were high up on the list. Only bereavement and divorce came higher. We thought that our move to Elgin was going to be straightforward as we were quite certain of the rightness of this change in Alistair's work. He had previously been a minister in the Free Church of Scotland, working as assistant minister in the Free North Church in Inverness. Although we were very happy there, as he talked with Dr Andrew McGowan about the possibility of setting up a theological school in the Highlands he began to feel himself drawn in that direction. Alistair had always enjoyed academia and was working towards a PhD. He became involved in the planning of the College and taught in it for a year on a part time basis. Then, as the College expanded and was able to support a full time New Testament lecturer, he felt very sure of his calling to this work. After an interview he was accepted and started work on the first of August 1996, our seventh wedding anniversary.

We started house hunting as soon as we knew that Alistair had got the job. Several people encouraged us to stay in Inverness for a while with Alistair commuting to Elgin, but we felt very strongly that as the Free Church in Elgin was small and without a minister we would be of more use there than in Inverness. The first day we went house hunting we found our dream home. It was an old cottage in Lossiemouth with five bedrooms and two living rooms. There was so much we could have done with it. Even a Granny flat would have been possible. Although the price would stretch us to the limit, we felt that we could just manage it. We put in an offer, it was accepted, and I bought two ceramic dolphins to put in our new bathroom to celebrate! The survey had shown that there was a bit of damp in one of the ceilings. It was probably just a loose slate, but to be on the safe side we got a slater to inspect the roof. His report was not good. An entirely new roof was needed at a cost of a further £6,000. That placed it well beyond our means. Fortunately we were able to withdraw our offer.

So it was back to the drawing board. Time was running out and I was in the final stages of pregnancy. We felt we needed a four bedroom house because Alistair needed a study. There was only one that fitted the bill, that was in our price range. It was in the centre of a large council estate. The one thing that I did not want was to move into a large estate of any kind. Although the house itself was fine it could not have been more different from our dream house in Lossiemouth. In my stressed state of mind I found it very hard to be positive about moving. I knew that I should be grateful for such a lovely house, but somehow knowing that seemed to make me feel even more resentful towards it.

We had a lot of help with the move and within days there were no boxes left in sight. So determined was I to have everything perfect that common sense seemed to vanish. I am not good at pacing myself, tending to do everything that can be done ... now. And that is not always for the best. Alistair was not unaffected. Once or twice over these difficult days he had even snapped at the girls. He is usually such a placid easy going man and always in control of the situation, but tiredness got to him too. I feel he is our stability as a family. Even when I am fraught and grumpy with the children he is always the same, calm and loving. But now he too had changed. And that brought me an added feeling of failure. Someone once said, 'Stop the world, I want to get off!' That was just how we felt. It was little wonder that Rachel was taking time to settle at school. I understood the tension on her face as I waved goodbye to her that morning. It probably reflected my own. How much worse we would both have felt had we known that we would not see each other again for a week.

As a teacher I had often seen the little ones in my care find it hard to cope with the noise and the rough and tumble of schools. But they had to learn. They had to toughen up. But now I stood at the school door with my heart rent in two. I wanted to protect her from every hurtful or frightening experience, and yet these days I was often the cause of these experiences.

Iris and I walked home together slowly. I was desperate to run on ahead to get everything ready but Iris could only manage a few slow painful steps at a time. She was determined that she would take her granddaughter to school every day until it was no longer physically possible. And she did. Iris died a year later, having walked her granddaughter to school on the Thursday she passed away in the early hours of Monday morning. At the gate, Iris stooped down to kiss my fretful son. 'Let me know how you get on,' she said as we parted company. I hurried indoors to get ready to see the doctor, and Iris went for a sleep.

But Not Alone

'Don't go!' I screamed from in my heart.
'Don't leave me alone.
I'm scared,
I'm not ready for this.
I'm not brave and strong,
I'm not old and wise.
I don't know what is wrong.

Don't go! Please don't go!
I'm still a child,
Not to the eyes of the world
But in my heart.
I need your strength
And your wisdom.
I need to know sense.

Don't go! My love!
I feel that I am torn in two.
You are my courage and my strength.
You are my wisdom
And my understanding.
How will I cope without you?
Please don't keep on going.

But as soon as the door shut,
I grew up!
You are still my tower
And my strength.
But I too can find courage and wisdom
From God alone
When I need it most.'

3

'Stephen Wilson!' the receptionist called. I picked Stephen up in his car chair and, with Bethany trailing along behind, made my way to the consulting room. With a smile the doctor motioned to me to sit down.

'I was wondering if I could give Stephen some Calpol,' I said. 'He has a high temperature and hasn't really slept or fed in over twelve hours. All he does is whimper and jerk. I'm sure that there is nothing really wrong but I just wanted to check.'

The doctor stripped him, examined him, and gave him some paracetamol to try and bring down his raging temperature.

'I'm going to put you in an examination room for a while,' he said. 'I'll see another patient then come back and see if the paracetamol has had any effect.'

He left the room. I looked at my tiny son lying on the big examination bed. His skin was pale and blotchy. It was what we as children called 'Gypsy tartan', except for the bright red patches on his face caused by constant screaming. I stroked his head. It was so hot. I stroked his plump little arms, holding on to his limp fingers. I stroked his tummy, his legs, his feet. His feet! Suddenly, my mouth was dry and my heart thumped hard against my chest. Tears of fear welled up in my eyes. His feet had turned black and scarlet! All sorts of thoughts came into my head. Had the blood supply been cut off from his feet? Would he have to have his feet amputated? As if hearing my silent scream the doctor appeared at the door.

He felt Stephen's skin and looked at his feet.

'Take him to the children's ward in Dr Gray's Hospital,' he said quietly. 'I'll phone them to let them know that you're coming. It is only precautionary, probably just for 24 hours observation. But I think that it's for the best.'

What was I to do with Rachel? She was only in school for the morning. I went to see Iris before going to the hospital. She agreed to take Rachel after school until I could come home for her. I would be able to leave Stephen in the hospital and come back to look after the girls. He wouldn't know if I was there or not. We went to the hospital which was only five minutes drive from the house. As I thought I would not have to stay long I didn't think that there was any need to pack a bag to take with me.

On arrival we were taken into a side room off the main children's ward. Stephen, who was fast asleep by now, was placed in a cot still in his car chair in an effort not to disturb him. And while we waited for a doctor to come to see him a nurse asked me the necessary questions. I struggled to think clearly through the jumble of fear and confusion that was filling my brain. 'Is Stephen spelt with a ph or a v?' 'Ph I think!' 'What's his date of birth?' I couldn't even remember today's date let alone what month he was born in, far less the date! 'What is your address?' 'What is your telephone number?' It usually takes me about two years to remember that and we had only been there for seven weeks. 'When did he first take ill?' The questions floated around my head. I tried hard to make sense of them and to answer them, but all I wanted to do was to hug my ill child very close to my body, all the better to comfort us both.

The doctor came. She was lovely; young with long dark hair and a gentle nature, she reminded me of a dear Edinburgh friend and I felt an instant trust in her. After looking briefly at Stephen she said that she would send him for a chest X-ray and call the consultant. This was all routine, she assured me. The consultant would want to see him, and would probably arrange to do a lumbar puncture. It is all routine, she said again. I felt a wrench as she left our ward. I had hoped that she would stay with me but I was to get used to talking to many people, and telling our story over and over again.

I will always remember seeing Stephen lying naked on that big X-ray table, with his little arms stretched up behind his head. He looked so sweet, so round and chubby. We used to laugh and say that he had no sharp corners. Every part of his little dimpled body was well covered with flesh. 'I've made a mistake,' I thought to myself. 'He's better now. It was all my imagination. Why am I putting him through this?' He looked so healthy. I comforted myself with the thought that the doctors would soon realise that he was alright and send us home.

We returned to the ward to find the consultant waiting for us. I felt so much happier in myself, but that was to be short-lived. The consultant looked at Stephen, and after yet more questions said, 'It's just routine, but I would like to do a lumbar puncture to rule out meningitis. It's probably not, but we must be sure. Are you happy for us to do that?'

Happy wasn't the word that I would have used but I was willing for them to do whatever they thought was necessary to make my baby well again. A shiver ran through me but I brushed it aside. It wasn't likely to be meningitis. Things like that don't affect my family. They only hit people who appear in newspapers. And that was usually because they had died. Of course I had heard about it on the television and in the papers, and I had listened to the advice given to parents regarding the symptoms, but somehow those warnings hadn't really touched reality. We have silly problems in our family like feet that are too wide to buy shoes for, but not life threatening illnesses like meningitis.

Stephen was immediately whisked away and I was left wondering how I was going to manage the day. If I were to stay with Stephen I would need help with the girls. But I had not yet met many people in Elgin whom I could ask, and I didn't have the phone numbers with me of those I felt I could. They were in my handbag and I had left it at home. But a friend who was coming for coffee that afternoon had given me her phone number written on an old Christmas card and that was still in my jacket pocket. I asked if I could use the phone and dialled Kate's number. Her answering machine was on and I left a message. 'Stephen has been taken into hospital, don't come for coffee. I'll phone when I can.' I never thought to say which hospital he was in or why he was there. Then I phoned my mother-in-law. Again all I got was her answering machine. 'Are you able to come through to Elgin to help me with the girls?' I asked, praying that it was her day off work. 'Stephen has been taken into hospital.'

A short while later, a nurse came into the playroom where I was playing with Bethany.

'There is a Kate on the phone,' she said. 'She wants to know if you are here. I can't give out that kind of information without your consent. What should I tell her?'

'Tell her "Yes!"' I cried. Within twenty minutes Kate was with me in the hospital. We had not known each other for long. A couple of months before we moved to Elgin she and her husband had wandered into the church in Inverness where my husband was working. They were not regular churchgoers, but we had got talking and instantly hit it off. And they had just moved to Forres, a town about twenty five miles from Inverness. As soon as we knew we were moving to Elgin, just twelve miles from Forres, we phoned them and invited them to church. They have been coming ever since and, with their family, they have filled the church with such a richness. But I will never cease to marvel at how God arranged that meeting months before so that when we were new to a town, knowing no-one and with a very ill child, we were provided for with such caring and self-sacrificing love.

Kate was sitting with me when the doctor called me through to the ward. We were laughing over the antics of Bethany and her little son Neil who were about the same age.

'We have done the lumbar puncture,' he said, 'and the spinal fluid that we drew out is cloudy. I'm afraid your son has bacterial meningitis.' I felt as though I had just crashed into a brick wall. Cold coursed it's way down through my body. Tears began flowing. I had managed to convince myself that this had all been a mistake. Surely the doctor would come back and tell me that it was just one of these innocent childhood viruses. Although I had been warned the reality had not sunk in. I had been in such a rush that morning that I didn't even have a hanky with me. As I wiped away my tears and my dripping nose with my bare hands I didn't care about the indignity of it. My son was perhaps dying!

'We have set up a drip,' the doctor continued. 'Don't be alarmed when you see him because we had to site the drip into his head. It was the only place that we could get a line in. We tried several other sites but his veins kept collapsing. There is a plastic cup secured over the needle because we can't take the risk of it being dislodged on the journey. He has also got heart monitors on, a blood pressure cuff and an oxygen level monitor. It will look very frightening, but they are all necessary. With all meningitis patients it's the policy that they are treated in Aberdeen. An ambulance is on its way to take us there now.'

I felt as if a wave was sweeping me along. Suddenly I was out of control. I didn't want to go to Aberdeen. I didn't want to leave my girls and my home. They needed me. I needed time ... time to think ... time to prepare. But the wave kept sweeping me along faster and faster out of control.

Stumbling through to the play room I ran for refuge to Kate's arms.

'It's meningitis,' I sobbed.

'Oh Jenny!' she breathed, holding me tight. 'I'm so sorry. Don't worry about the children. I'll look after them until Granny gets here. Give me your car keys and I'll get David to take it home for you.'

I needed to make one more phone call. Alistair's Mum had bought him a pager watch for his birthday. It had come in useful many times before when I had needed to get hold of him and he had been out visiting members of the congregation, but today it paid for itself. I paged him with a message to phone home urgently. It crossed my mind that when he did he might not get any answer. But I had to leave that in God's hands.

Then Stephen in his little cot and with wires everywhere, the doctor, a nurse and myself, were ushered into an ambulance by two men in green boiler suits. I watched Elgin disappear as the ambulance, with it's blue light flashing, sped towards Aberdeen. I had no great love for the place that had taken me away from Inverness and my beloved friends but it held my other two children, and already I was missing them and anxious about how they would cope with being separated from me for the first time in their lives. It was ironic really that I had given birth to Stephen at home, partly because I did not want to leave the girls, and partly because I didn't like being in hospital. And now, just eight weeks later, I was leaving them and hospital was to become my home for I didn't know how long. God did. And he was able to use even this trauma to give me the rest I so much needed. But my tiredness was the last thing on my mind as we sped towards Aberdeen.

Mother

Sleep closed my eyes,
And I entered that deep
Swirling world of unconsciousness,
My body grew weightless
As sleep dragged it down
Slowly,
Through the waters.

But then a cry!
Without a conscious thought I was awake.
In an instant I had emerged
From the tides of sleep.
That cry was for me.
I felt my milk begin to flow,
My arms ached to cradle the precious life
That had been given to me.
But I had no place in this room!

Angels in white fluttered to and fro
Ministering to my child.
And I stood in uneasy stillness
My back against the wall
And watched, as my child,
Who was given to me for help,
And protection,
For nurturing and nourishment,
Was cared for by strangers.
And it hurt!

A sea of tears emerged.
And I was tossed on the storms of frustration
And guilt.
My body cried out for sleep,
But my hurting mind
Would not let the healing waves
Wash over me.

4

The two hour long drive to Aberdeen seemed to last for ever. Although the motion of the ambulance and the gentle 'beep beep' of the monitors made me feel sleepy, and my body screamed out for sleep, I could not rest until I knew what was happening to Stephen. I was so grateful to the doctor and nurse who accompanied us. They were friendly and chatty and kept a close eye on their tiny patient. So that he could constantly monitor his condition, the doctor sat on the floor of the ambulance. Stephen was completely motionless. Not a whimper. Not a cry. His skin was pale and blotchy and his eyes were tight shut. He did not feel like my baby as he lay there.

To help pass the time the doctor and nurse talked about the beautiful new hospital that we had in Elgin and of how nice it was to work there. The corridors were wide, the rooms large and bright. Pictures hung in airy reception areas and bright carpets finished it off with style. What a shock I was in for when I arrived in Aberdeen Sick Children's Hospital. Following Stephen's cot, which was tied with all the monitors on to an ambulance stretcher, through dark claustrophobic corridors to his small room, I felt as if I was being taken to the centre of the earth.

His cramped little room contained a tiny cot, a chair, sink and a bedside cupboard. There was just space for three adults standing very close together in the middle of the furniture and nothing else. I stayed outside while the doctors and nurses transferred him to the cot and did all the necessary checks, aware of the other parents looking at our little procession, wondering what our story was. As I looked back at them we were immediately united in pain. Looks of understanding and helplessness passed between us. I longed to be in the big ward with them but, because of the nature of Stephen's illness, I was not allowed in the ward and they were not allowed in our little room. I could just look longingly at my comrades through the glass window which divided us.

My sleeping quarters were in a wing adjacent to the ward. They were very comfortable. At first I was dismayed to find that I had to share with another woman but I never saw her face as we went to our room just to sleep and often when we arrived the light was already switched off. Not wanting to disturb each other, we undressed in the darkness and slid silently between the sheets. But we talked for hours through the long dark stretches of the night, about our fears and our hopes, our worries and frustrations and eventually our joys.

If the phone rang during the night it was the ward sister wanting one of us to return to the ward to settle our child. It was a comfort being able to sleep, knowing they were being looked after and if they needed us we could be called in an instant. I remember many trips through the hospital in the early hours of the morning wearing a pair of striped pink pyjamas I bought from the hospital shop. They were far too big round the waist and too short in the leg. I had also bought some blue spotted slippers. The first time that I wore my new attire I felt very self-conscious until I bumped into my clone coming towards me down the corridor. 'I see you shop in the same boutique!' she smiled.

When I returned to the ward, having seen my sleeping quarters, Stephen was lying motionless in his cot. Because his temperature had plummeted dramatically he was wrapped in a shiny silver blanket. Several machines gave off constant bleeps and every now and again a siren would sound from one of them. A nurse sat by his side constantly monitoring him and making notes. Her name was Liz, and she was to be Stephen's main nurse. I felt useless and empty and tired. A nurse popped her head round the door.

'Your husband has just been on the phone. He is catching a flight from Manchester airport and will get into Aberdeen at 7:30 pm.'

Alistair had managed to contact someone!

His pager had bleeped just south of Killintone Lake Service Station not long after they had had a stop there. They thought at first that it was a joke. The year before, when they had been doing a similar trip to Wales, I bleeped him to ask if he could take a wedding in a ruined castle, for a colleague who had just fallen off a roof and badly broken his leg. They had joked about what other messages I could have for him. But, remembering Stephen's condition, they decided to stop as soon as possible just in case there was a real problem. When they found somewhere to stop the phone was engaged. When he did eventually get through, Alistair was surprised to hear Kate's voice at the other end. She told him all she knew, and said that she thought that he should try to come home.

While Kate and Alistair were still speaking his mum arrived at the house. She had found the message on her answering machine and, not being able to contact me, had come straight to our house in Elgin. Being a nurse, she tried to explain to Alistair the gravity of the situation without alarming him too much. She agreed that he should come home quickly. But how? The nearest train station was Lancaster. Driving there as fast as they could they discovered that the next train didn't leave until very late that night.

One of Alistair's colleagues came up with the idea of getting him to an airport and flying him home. He phoned ahead to Manchester airport to see if there were any available seats on the next flight. Finding that there were, he made a reservation. The airline staff appreciated the gravity of the problem and agreed to process Alistair's ticket as soon as he arrived. The call to the airport was not the only one that was made. Alistair's colleagues phoned their families, churches and praying friends, asking them to pray for Stephen's recovery. Within a couple of hours of Stephen being admitted to hospital, hundreds of people all over Great Britain, many of whom we had never even met, were praying for our tiny son. We heard of many impromptu prayer meetings. One even took place in a school staff room at lunch time.

The news was passed on to the prayer meeting in our former church in Inverness. One of the members told me that she will always remember the moment that they were told. A chilled silence settled on the congregation as they took in the news and then heads all through the room bowed as each individual prayed for this tiny life. Most of them had never even met him because we left just one week after he was born. I don't think that I had ever before fully appreciated the enveloping love and the closeness of the family of Christ.

I often reflect on that time and wonder if our churches would be stronger places if we were more aware of the trials and hurts of those around us. Maybe the all too common trivial bickering and fighting over things that are not worth the weight of time would cease if we prayed earnestly and worked together for what was important. It would be wrong to say that through their prayers all my worries vanished, but I did, throughout that time that was fraught with pain and anguish, sense that there was a controlling hand helping me cope. I didn't need to be in control because that was the job of my Heavenly Father. What a lot I learned then about resting in his arms and letting him take over.

But for Alistair it was all activity, for it was a mad rush in the minibus to get him to the airport to catch his flight. They arrived just on time only to be met outside the airport by a traffic jam. Abandoning the minibus they ran to the terminal, arriving well after the flight had been called. The departure lounge was empty but, because the staff were aware of the situation, Alistair was able to join the flight without any problems and without having to give any explanations. While he was in the air, another of his colleagues had got hold of a friend in Aberdeen who agreed to pick Alistair up from the airport and drive him to the hospital. Lewis and his family were very good to him, opening up their home to him, while he stayed in Aberdeen.

Eight o'clock arrived, and I heard Alistair's voice coming down the corridor. He was grey and close to tears. In our eight years of married life I had never seen Alistair cry.

'I thought ....,' he began. 'I thought I wouldn't make it in time ....'

I gathered him into my arms.

'We don't even have a photograph of him,' he sobbed.

I was stunned! We didn't! In all our busyness of moving and settling into our new home we hadn't taken one picture of our new born child. We had hundreds of the girls and not one of Stephen!

The monitors kept a constant bleep. Numbers and lights flashed, nurses came and went and we stood, almost too numb to speak. My head pounded. My neck was stiff. I asked one of the nurses if I could have some painkillers.

'You'll have to go to A&E to get some,' she

said. 'I can't give you anything until a doctor has checked you out.'

They thought that I might have meningitis too! Of course, Stephen had to have caught it from someone, and who was more likely than his mother? We walked across to the A&E department. My head was spinning thinking of all the implications that would have. Surely not! How much could we as a family be asked to bear? After a brief examination, I was given two tablets and told to go to bed.

Yes, bed was just what I needed. It had been a long and stressful day.

Before Alistair left that night, I asked him for a shirt from out of his suitcase so that I would have something clean to wear the following day. He took one out and handed it to me. It was all crumpled up. I had never got round to doing the ironing!

Tears

Tears of frustration
Tears of pain
Tear at my heart again and again.
But with the hurt
And with the cries
The healing salt runs from my eyes.

He feels my hurt
He feels my pain,
He longs to grant me joy again.
He hung in agony
And as he died,
The healing salt ran from his eyes.

But tears of sorrow
And tears of pain,
Won't for ever with me remain,
For through his love
And through his grace
Tears of joy flow down my face.

5

Alistair came early the next day and together we met with the consultant. Things could still go either way, we were warned. Because Stephen had been given the all important antibiotics quickly he stood a good chance of recovery, although there was no room for complacency. We were told wc should be very grateful to our GP for his prompt assessment of the situation. So many children, especially babies, with meningitis are overlooked because it is such a difficult illness to diagnose. About one in ten babies who catch the illness die. The key to a successful recovery is the speed in which the antibiotics are administered.

On the hospital walls was a list of what to look out for.

Children – Stiff neck   Dislike of light
    Nausea   Drowsiness   Rash
Babies – Whimpering or screaming
    Blotchy skin   Rash   Refusal to
    feed   Dislike of being handled

I have since noticed the same poster in the entrance of Rachel's school. But, as with so many things, you take no notice of it until it happens to you or someone you know. And you never think it will. I had been so worried about being one of the troublesome patients who disturb their doctor during the night that I had ignored what my heart was telling me about my son. But nobody knows a child like a parent does. We knew Stephen was a placid baby and that it was quite unlike him to be so disturbed. When things are so obviously wrong we must listen to our hearts rather than the posters on the surgery wall. Delay in seeking medical attention can, in the case of meningitis, have fatal consequences. I know from speaking to a friend who is a GP that doctors do get called out for very trivial things, but if a baby or young child is displaying worrying symptoms we should never take the risk of waiting until morning.

The doctor talked us through what would probably happen over the next few days and what signs to look out for. He explained the hospital procedures and gave us as much advice as he could about caring for our son. I must have appeared over-optimistic after his talk because he went to great pains to warn me against becoming complacent, telling us that Stephen wasn't by any means over the worst yet. Because of the risk of swelling to his head he was not allowed any fluids for a couple of days, and even then his fluid intake was restricted. Every hour his head circumference was measured to gauge how much fluid was there. His nappies was numbered, and I thought at first that this was to prevent any being stolen, after all the government was cutting back on extra expense in the National Health Service! But an amused nurse explained that each nappy was weighed before it was put on Stephen, and weighed when it was taken off, so measuring all that went in and came out!

As a result of Stephen's fluid restriction, and also because he was too ill to suck, I could not breast-feed him. I tried to keep my milk supply going by using a breast pump, and soon had quite a collection of bottles of milk in the hospital freezer ready for when he could feed again. But I ended up with thrush and, persevere as I did, I could not resume the feeding adequately when he was better. Having fed the girls for about ten months, I was disappointed to have to stop feeding Stephen after only two. Later, when we were settled back home, the health visitors were quite amused at my struggles to resume breast-feeding. 'Most of our mums are trying to cut out the feeding by this time and you are trying to increase it!' they laughed. But it didn't work and soon I had to accept that he would just have to be a happy bottle fed baby.

We agreed that Alistair should go back to Inverness where the girls were staying with his mum. She had picked them up from our house where Kate had been looking after them. Kate, who is both practical and thoughtful, emptied the cupboards and fridge of perishable foods, dried the wet clothes in the washing machine and packed bags for the girls and for me. Unfortunately most of the clothes she packed for me were still too small as I had not yet gone back to my pre-pregnancy size! So, until I was able to manage a trip to the shops, I had to make do with Alistair's crumpled shirt. Before leaving Kate made the beds, tidied up the house and made sure that everything was left in good order.

It was late afternoon on the day Stephen was transferred to Aberdeen, that Edna, Alistair's mum, took the children to Inverness. Iain, Alistair's dad, also came through to help because they were unsure if it would be easier to look after the children in our home or theirs. It didn't take Edna long to realise she would never be able to find where everything was in our house. At that point neither could I! So they decided to take the girls to Inverness.

Rachel travelled with her Grandad and

Bethany went in Granny's car. Bethany was so tired that she fell asleep before they even left Elgin. And she remained sound, despite the discomfort of her head wobbling around as she was only restrained with a seat belt. She didn't even wake when her Granny stopped the car to make her more comfortable. And tiredness wasn't Bethany's only problem. On reaching Inverness she found a packet of cough sweets in Edna's pocket and started to eat them without even taking off the wrappers. She was starving. The poor wee lass hadn't eaten since breakfast time!

The one essential that had been overlooked was Bethany's dummy. She loved stroking a tag and sucking her dummy. Not long before we had left Inverness, when I took Rachel to her nursery class, Bethany ran in with her sister, sucking her dummy and stroking a tag which was attached to some green material. Any clothing tag would do Bethany. If she found anything lying about with a tag on it, she picked it up and stroked it. The nursery teachers laughed when they saw her that day. I soon discovered why. To my immense embarrassment she was stroking the tag on a pair of Alistair's underpants!

Alistair's brother and sister-in-law, Andrew and Eilidh, were also called in to help. Eilidh volunteered to take the children to buy Bethany a new selection of dummies, although I think that the treats went a bit further than that! Bethany, satisfied, fell asleep quickly that night. But Rachel, who worries about things, found it harder to settle. At four she was just becoming aware of life and death. When Alistair took his first funeral Rachel, who was two at the time, wanted to know all about what daddy was doing. We told her that a Christian lady had died, that her soul had gone to be with Jesus and that daddy was going to bury her body. Later that day we found her with lots of cushions and blankets around her. 'What are you doing?' we asked. Her answer took us aback. 'I'm burying my botty like daddy did to that lady!' Not long before Stephen's illness, Rachel had her preschool booster injection. And one of her concerns was that Stephen was having to have injections. Rachel is a very caring child, and her love for her baby brother was very touching. Even now she cares for him in a very special way.

We had never spent a night away from the girls before. That, combined with the general upheaval of the past two months, made us decide that Alistair should leave me with Stephen in Aberdeen and go to be with them. He travelled to Inverness, stayed with his parents for the night, then took the children back to Elgin. And for Rachel that meant back to school. School was proving difficult enough for her without a prolonged absence from it. Once again, and with a heavy heart, I said goodbye to my husband.

Loneliness invaded every inch of my body. Up till then I hadn't cried. There hadn't been the time. Because everything had happened so suddenly it had brought with it a feeling of unreality. But when Alistair left and I found myself alone again, the dreadful reality of the situation flooded through me. I felt so alone. And it was then I cried. Most of that day and the next was spent in tears. Time was heavy on my hands. There was nothing for me to do but sleep, watch my baby struggling for life, and cry. Picking up the Gideon Bible from beside Stephen's cot, I tried to read it. But, try as I might, I couldn't settle my mind to concentrate.

Yet once again I was to see the goodness of the Lord in providing people to help me. Mum, who was unable to come to be with us because of another family trauma, phoned Mr Philip, my minister in Glasgow some time before. Mrs Philip contacted her nephew and his wife in Aberdeen. Rebecca, came to the hospital as soon as she could and talked and prayed with me. She brought some fruit, a radio cassette player, some music and toiletries, guessing I might need them. How right she was. I had arrived in Aberdeen without a toothbrush or even a change of underwear! Among her gifts was a shower gel called Dewberry. That night I had the best shower of my entire life. As I stood under the warm spray of water, with the heavy scent of the shower gel filling my breath, I was suddenly filled with an overwhelming sense of peace and relaxation. Even now if I smell it I relive that beautiful moment.

Another provision of friendship came through a social worker. My friend, Nina, knowing that Karen often worked in the hospital, phoned and asked her to visit me and give me a hug. She arrived at nine o'clock that night. As visitors were not generally allowed in at that time, she wore her official hospital badge and asked if she could see me for a while. The staff let her in and she became a frequent visitor to our little room. No-one ever questioned her presence, until one day when she arrived while I was at the canteen having lunch. 'Your social worker was here while you were away,' a nurse reported when I returned. 'Would you like me to phone the Social Work Department and tell them that they can send someone down now?' I had to confess that she was not my social worker, just a friend. I often wondered what they thought I had done to deserve visits three times a day and in the evening from a social worker!

The next thing that I had to face was a visit from the Communicable Diseases Officer. She checked Stephen, looking closely at the rash that had developed on his right arm. Again I had to go through the list of events of the previous few days. Then I had to write down the names, addresses and doctors of everyone who had held or kissed Stephen in the previous seven days. That was some job! We had been to a birthday party where about fifteen children were present. Their mums had all taken it in turns to nurse and admire Stephen. Also we had visited several of our Inverness friends and on Sunday we had been to church.

About forty people were considered to have been at enough risk to be contacted by the Communicable Diseases Officer. They all needed to be treated with strong antibiotics, either to kill the bacteria that causes meningitis if one of them was the carrier, or to prevent them from catching it. We will never know who Stephen caught it from. Some 52% of us carry the bacteria around in our throats and are quite unaware of its presence. It is not known why occasionally in some people it develops into meningitis. The antibiotics had unpleasant side effects. They turned all bodily fluids fluorescent red! When we cried, our tears were red. When we went to the toilet, our urine was red. And when we cleaned our teeth, our saliva was red. We all had a couple of fluorescent red days!

Andrew and Eilidh, Iain and Edna, all had to take the antibiotics too. There was a great deal of hilarity over going to the toilet. They would argue about who would go first, none of them wanting to have this red experience. 'How was it for you?' they asked each other. 'Fluorescent red!' would be the reply. Eilidh laughed so much that it brought tears to her eyes. Of course, much to everyone's amusement, her tears were red too! Other side effects were more unpleasant: nausea, hot flushes, dizziness and palpitations. Maybe the men will be a bit more understanding of women's hot flushes after experiencing them for themselves!

Iris, our next door neighbour had to contend with all of that as well as her chemotherapy. Not wanting to worry her granddaughter unnecessarily she didn't tell her about the possible side effects, thinking that they might not affect her. At school the next day Heather's teacher heard a scream coming from the girls toilets. She had just been to the toilet and thought that she was bleeding! Because the school hadn't been informed of this possibility there was a panic until a phone call home put everyone's minds at rest.

As Stephen lay there in his cot, he had no idea what an effect he was having on so many lives and in so many different ways!

Beating For Me

From the depths of my heart
I cried,
But the pounding of my heart
Must have been too loud,
For you didn't seem to hear.

My heart missed a beat!
In the silence
My very soul called out,
But you must have missed it.
For you didn't seem to hear.

The tiny bleeping of the monitors
The shallow almost nonexistent breaths
That didn't yet know how to shout
Were in their very being a cry to the living God.
But you didn't seem to hear.

But through the turmoil
And through the pain
A strong but gentle beating could be heard.
Not that of my crying heart,
Or that of a struggling heart,
But that of my Father's heart
Beating for me.

6

During my long hours of waiting at Stephen's cotside I yearned for the company of Christians. Having prayed that one of the nurses might be a believer I was delighted to see Liz, Stephen's special nurse, wearing a praying hands badge on her lapel.

'Are you a Christian?' I asked hopefully during one of her visits.

'That depends what you mean by a Christian,' came the reply.

'Well I saw the praying hands on your lapel,' I said.

'Oh that!' she said. 'It was given to me by a friend a long time ago. I reckon that if I have got God on my shoulder, I can't go far wrong!'

I felt as though someone had kicked me in the teeth.

Needing a fellow Christian to talk to and pray with I went in search of the hospital chaplain. Surely he would understand my view on life. The chapel, when I found it, was deserted. An hour later I tried again, and an hour after that. Still there was no-one around. When I looked for a note of open hours, services or times when I could meet the chaplain, the only information

I could find was the schedule of Muslim prayer meetings! I should have asked the nursing staff about the chaplain, but somehow in my confused state I never thought of the obvious.

For a lot of my day I sat listening to tapes of psalms and meditating over them. The psalmist had never sat by the hospital bedside of a sick son or daughter, but he had known suffering in a way that I have only touched the surface of, and through that suffering he had come into a deeper and fuller relationship with God. And I thought of God sending his own Son, Jesus, to die for us. My pain was because my child might die. I realised that God too experienced such pain, but not only that, he also had the pain of having chosen that his child should go through death. And he did all that for me. He knew what I was feeling. When I looked to others for help in places where I felt sure that help would be, I found none. But I could always call on my Lord, day or night, and he heard not just my prayers but the tormented groans from my soul, as I watched my son going through so many painful experiences.

Find rest, O my soul, in God alone;
my hope comes from him.
He alone is my rock and my salvation;
he is my fortress, I shall not be shaken.

My salvation and my honour depend on God;
he is my mighty rock, my refuge.
Trust in him at all times, O people;
pour out your hearts to him,
for God is our refuge.

Psalm 62:5-8

Once, while listening to a tape, the nursery nurse came in. She threw up her hands in mock horror. 'Can I not get away from religion anywhere?' she asked. 'Through in the big ward they are playing some Muslim music and in here it is Christian music! Do you think that someone is trying to tell me something?' I answered her with a weak smile, unable to say anything for fear of yet another rejection. But something inside me made me question how she had recognised the Ian White psalms so quickly. By the end of the week, as I got to know her better, I discovered that she was in fact a Christian. If only I had persisted in my quest I would have been able to talk a bit more freely about my feelings with her. I am sure that I was not alone in giving up so easily but the deprivation I felt as a result has made me realise the need to be open about my faith.

Every four hours, through both day and night, a nurse came to give Stephen his intravenous antibiotics. Because he was so ill his veins kept collapsing and they were constantly looking for new sites to put a line in. One day it took the doctors eighteen attempts to site a line. For nearly an hour they tried to insert a needle as I sat in agony hearing him screaming at the pain of it. It was the only time during those first few days that he made any noise at all. The rest of the time he just lay motionless in his cot. On that day a friend was visiting. I struggled to carry on a conversation with her, all the while listening with increasing frustration to Stephen's haunting cries from the treatment room. Was there nothing I could do to help my son? Eventually Liz, Stephen's special nurse, marched into the treatment room and picked him up, telling the doctors that he had had enough and she was going to call the consultant. As his screaming stopped I explained the situation to my visitor and said goodbye. My only thoughts were to comfort my child.

It seemed ironic that at times I cried out for the company of Christians, yet when I did have visitors I couldn't bear to be away from Stephen. No one apart from close family was allowed into his little room. When next I saw him his tiny head had been shaved on each side and over the top, and there were needle holes all over his body. My stomach lurched. Every instinct was to take him up in my arms and leave the hospital, distancing him from all this pain. But somewhere within me sense prevailed. The mortality rate for untreated bacterial meningitis is 100%. When the consultant came he managed to site a temporary line which stuck out at a very precarious angle from his foot. Stephen's slightest movement, or a bump from one of the nurses doing his observations, would dislodge the line. He promised me that the next day they would take him to theatre and site a permanent one.

After the pain of watching Stephen suffering so much, I sat looking down at the mass of cables and wires that sought to hold my baby down. How I longed to tear them off and grasp my precious son close to my chest. His chubby little dimpled arms and legs hid the full seriousness of his illness. People talk about the 'Big C'. We were now facing the 'Big M': the illness that most parents fear and dread, but nobody thinks will ever happen in their family.

Time stood still. The world outside the four walls no longer seemed to exist. This was life. Or was it death?

The gentle beeping of the monitors was suddenly interrupted by a shrill, piercing sound. It brought the nurses running from their station. I pressed my back against the cold, hard wall, making room for these angels in white.

'You little imp!' one of the nurses laughed, looking down at my son.

'My son is dying, and she calls him an imp!' I wanted to scream at her and tell her to go away. But she moved, allowing me to see my little imp.

'You didn't like that needle in your foot did you?' she asked my baby gently.

Then I saw ... his big bright eyes were trying desperately to focus on the mobile above his cot! Oh how beautiful those eyes were. So clear and blue. So alive!

My heart stopped, missed a beat. For a moment I forgot to breathe, then tears spilled from my eyes. First I touched my little cherub, oh so gently. Then I longed to scoop him up, to feel his life, to kiss him all over. But those wires! 'Let me help you,' the nurse said, understanding the burning emotions that raged through my body. I pressed him tight to me, not wanting to put him back in that cot ever again. I could feel his little heart beating against my chest. The beat of life. His plump little tummy rose and fell against mine. My heart lifted in elation. Then he wriggled, struggling to be free of all that sought to hold him down. I looked at my son, the fighter, who against the odds was recovering from bacterial meningitis.

And not for the first time I was proud to be his mother. It seemed a lot longer than just five days ago, that I had sat on the sitting room floor crying. 'Lord! I can't cope. You've got to help me!'

God not only answered my prayers and those of the many other people who had been praying with us for Stephen's recovery, but there was a real working in unison with Christ and his people. These people prayed in faith, believing that God could heal. They were praying not just for Stephen's healing but for the whole family as we struggled through this time. And they prayed most of all for God's will to be done, whether through Stephen's healing or through his death. But why pray, when God had the answer already in his hands, when my Heavenly Father had known from the dawn of time what would happen to my son? I cannot pretend to know or understand the mind of God, but I believe that in the midst of our pain, I was able to catch a tiny glimpse of what prayer is about.

It is about talking to God, relying on him and acknowledging that there are things beyond our control. We have a great need to be in control of things: of our high powered jobs, busy family lives, and churches as they strive to reach out to the great unchurched majority. All these things are commendable, but sometimes we tend to forget the God part of the equation. But we are not in control, not in any real sense. And we don't like it because it is alien to today's way of thinking. If only we would grasp that God has the whole world in his hands and that we can only look to him, and plead with him for help. Without prayer we would never understand that pleading for something outside of our control, that only God can bring about. And we would never know the joy of seeing our prayers answered and knowing that God does hear us.

Another factor that was imprinted on my mind was that in prayer we work together. Many hundreds of people throughout the world were praying for our tiny little boy. We often say to our friends, 'We'll be thinking of you'. What good does thinking of somebody do? But to be able to say 'we are praying for you' means something. It means that God, who is so great and can do all things for his glory, is active in the situation. That makes us part of a greater whole, part of God's work joined across the continents. Miles and time are no object. And prayer works. I think of that day I cried to God in desperation, and he heard. I think of the prayers for Stephen's life that he heard and answered. 'Ask and you will receive, and your joy will be complete' (John 16:24).

I often think back to my pregnancies and the months that followed them with feelings of anger and frustration. As far as I understand in days gone by women were generally treated with added care almost to the point of suffocation. It was expected that women would remain in bed for quite some time after giving birth, and with the help of the extended family they would be given care and rest. Nowadays we are under a great deal of pressure to be super-women. Pregnancy, we are often reminded, is not an illness just a condition. We have to get on with our lives. But to most women pregnancy does bring sickness and other complications or discomforts which, if not associated with pregnancy, would be seen as an illness. We try to push on, pretending to cope as well as the next woman, suffering often in silence, not even telling our husbands how bad or tired we feel, lest they should not believe us or see us as some lesser being. We listen to stories of painless births and of women going about their daily business just hours after giving birth with no ill effects, and we feel like miserable failures. So we perpetuate the myth that pregnancy does not affect our lives.

It is hardly surprising then that so many of us suffer from post-natal depression to some extent or other. I have never been diagnosed as having post-natal depression but, looking back, at two of my three pregnancies I am fairly sure that I was suffering quite considerably. At the time I would not have admitted it to anyone, least of all myself. I remember not long after Rachel was born being awake through most of the night with our very fractious baby. We had just dropped off to sleep when the postman rang the door bell to deliver a parcel and yet more baby cards. As I opened the first card I saw the words, 'You have a girl to make your joy complete'. At that time of the morning I wasn't aware of any joy, just a lack of sleep. If I had had an open fire I would have thrown all of the cards on it. And my family were suffering too. Depression never affects just one person, yet it isolates all who are involved.

What a lot of courage it takes to admit that we are not coping with what is, after all, one of the most natural processes in life. But the more that I talk to other mothers the more that I am convinced that we must learn to be honest with each other. It is not until we are honest with others that they find it easy to be open with us, and unburden their hearts. Sharing is a great healer. Knowing that others have gone through this too, and being able to talk honestly without fear of being thought foolish or weak, can sometimes be the first step out of the darkness of depression. New mothers need to realise that they are not alone in their tiredness and frustrations, to be assured that they don't need to be superwomen.

Our bodies have been made as they are for a purpose. They tell us to rest, not to run about with the duster when the baby has gone to sleep. What we need is a sleep too. When we have little ones it is not the time to be organising this thing or that in the church, because we are 'not working, just looking after our children'. Being helpful and busy can be of great benefit to us, but only if we are able to cope with the demands it places upon us. And we must look at the stresses we place on our children. They are often the first ones to suffer when we are depressed or tired. If we are prepared to support others through the difficult times of childbirth and child rearing we must be honest in admitting when we are struggling and ask for help ourselves. As I look back to that time when I sat on the floor crying to God I am thankful that I had a God to cry to, but I wish that I had also had the courage to cry to others for help too. Our stay in hospital gave me time to think.

One of my sweetest memories of the time of Stephen's illness, was seeing my girls again for the first time since he and I were whisked away to Aberdeen without even saying goodbye. Alistair brought them to the hospital to visit. I heard their voices as they came along the corridor and flew the length of the ward to scoop them up in my arms. They were allowed to look through the window into his tiny room and watch him sleeping peacefully. Both girls were quite alarmed to see the remaining monitors attached to him, although most had been removed by this time. Having ready-made baby sitters in hospital, we went out for the day to Story Book Glen, an outdoor park with large life size models of nursery rhyme characters, which is situated just outside Aberdeen. The sense of freedom was wonderful. We didn't stand still the whole time. We ran, played chases, and climbed on everything that could be climbed on. Life was fun again, and so precious. And we held hands and laughed in a carefree way that we had not been able to do as a family for many months.

'Look at me Mummy,' Rachel shouted from inside Cinderella's coach. 'I'm a princess!' And as I looked at her gorgeous smiling face I felt that she and her little sister, who was trying to steal Baby Bear's porridge, were every bit as precious as any princesses could ever be. The scowls and tears of anger and frustration had gone as we realised anew what precious gifts we had in each other. If I could have bottled that day and sold it I would now be a rich woman.

And when they left to go home later that day, I felt ready to say goodbye. It was no longer with a heavy heart that I watched them go. Stephen was smiling, my children were happy, and it would only be a matter of days until I would be with Alistair again and we could be together.

Friends

I looked for a friend today.
Not one who would talk of the news or the
      weather,
Or one that would say
He was thinking of me,
But one with whom I could cry,
And would pray with me.

I looked for a friend today.
There were many people about.
They fed me and gave me books to read.
They said 'We're thinking about you,'
And then they left,
Without praying with me.

I looked for a friend today.
And you came, my love.
You saw I was tired, and my eyes were red,
You gave me a hug,
And you kissed my dirty face,
And you prayed with me.

7

When we returned to the hospital I was alarmed to find Stephen jerking again. His temperature had shot up and he was whimpering. The doctor was called immediately and he examined him. 'His recovery has almost been too quick,' he explained. 'Sometimes they do have slight relapses.' His head was measured and the monitors once more attached to his hands, arms and chest. Fortunately this was just a short-lived blip. By the next day he was once more well on his way to recovery. The nursery nurse started bringing toys for him to play with. Stephen became increasingly demanding as he longed for the cuddles and attention that he had been lacking. It was so nice to be able to sit with him on the rocking chair in that tiny room and give him time, without always feeling the need to rush about tidying the house or to iron more shirts! He had become quite a smiler and a delight to be with.

Tuesday morning came, eight days after we first arrived in Aberdeen. The doctor did his usual ward round with his group of nurses, student doctors and junior doctors. They all squeezed into our tiny room, overflowing out into the corridor but all trying to appear interested. I listened to the nurse's familiar introduction: 'This is Stephen Wilson aged eight weeks.' I remember wanting to shout out, 'He's nine weeks now!' That extra week was very important to me. 'He is here with bacterial meningitis.' After the preliminary discussions on Stephen's case, the room fell silent.

'Well, Mrs Wilson,' the doctor said in his gentle Australian accent with a sparkle in his eyes. 'How would you like to go home?'

'Home?' I repeated stupidly.

'Yes, home!' he said. 'You remember the place where you have to cook and wash dirty socks! Stephen doesn't need constant observations any more. He has pulled through and has overcome the meningitis. There is no reason why he can't finish his course of antibiotics at home under the care of your local GP.'

'When.....?' I stuttered.

He smiled. 'Today.'

I thanked him, wanting desperately to throw my arms around him. He had been so kind and friendly, even in his gentle reminders to me of how ill my son was and how realistic I had to be in my appraisal of the situation.

'Stephen has responded well to the treatment,' he said. 'I'm sure you will be glad never to have to see us again.'

Then the troop of medics left me to wonder how I was to get home. I flew to the telephone to tell Alistair the news. 'Can you come for us? Now?' I cried.

There was of course only one answer. Alistair collected Rachel from school and then the three of them drove as fast as the law would allow them, from Elgin to Aberdeen.

I returned to my room to start packing. First the awful pink stripey pyjamas I had bought from the hospital shop were folded neatly into a plastic carrier bag (they are now in the children's dressing up box, but rarely worn!), then my other hospital clothes followed. Soon the little room was emptied. My time here was coming to an end. In the midst of my excitement of going home, it suddenly struck me that I would no longer have the doctors and nurses to do everything for me. What if something went wrong and Stephen became ill again? What if I couldn't make him take his antibiotics? What if ... I sat on the bed in a blind panic. It was so safe here knowing that I wasn't in charge of the situation. Now, all of a sudden, that security was being taken away from me. Of course I was glad to be going home, but couldn't I just take one of the doctors with me? Then a voice inside me said, 'But you do have a doctor. I will never leave you or forsake you.

Trust in me.' My newly learned lesson of leaning on my Heavenly Father had already been rocked.

I walked back along to the ward. Stephen was playing happily with the ladybird mobile which hung above his cot. His cheeks were once more pink and rosy and his eyes bright and alert. He smiled at me as I entered his room. Although Stephen smiled a lot these days, his grins were never directed at Liz who always gave him his intravenous antibiotics. But today when she came in to give him his medicine, she removed his line as well.

'Well my wee man,' she said, smiling down at him. 'That's the last time that I will ever have to do that.'

'Congratulations!' she said, looking up at me. 'You must be so excited.'

'I am,' I told her honestly. 'But I'm also very nervous about how I am going to cope without having you and the doctors around. What if something goes wrong, and I don't know what to do? What if he won't take his medicine?'

'You'll find that the doctor and health visitor will probably visit you tomorrow,' Liz assured me. 'They'll be telephoned today to tell them of your homecoming. If you need them they are only a phone call away. And don't hesitate to phone them.'

I knew that it was true, but while we were here everything was safe. I didn't have to worry about everything. When Stephen had first become unwell, I hadn't even been aware of how ill he was. Would I know another time? I felt as Rachel must have done on her first day at school: frightened about taking that big step into the unknown, and leaving security behind.

It was so good to see Alistair and the girls again that evening and to walk out of the hospital with our family still complete. We could so easily have been leaving with one of its members missing. But God in his gracious wisdom knew that this was not the time. One of the first things that we did when we got home was to take photographs of Stephen and his sisters. The girls posed very proudly for pictures with their precious baby brother. Their love for him was so evident then, and it still is today. A special bond has been built between them. Stephen is of course still oblivious to the reasons, just seeing his sisters as ever willing playmates and friends. But young as the girls were at the time they have not, and I don't think ever will, forget that week when he was ill. Rachel is particularly proud of the fact that she had managed to get Stephen to sleep when he was ill and I could not. 'It's because you never thought to sing him a lullaby,' she told me.

We have had many laughs when we watch the children playing doctors and nurses with their friends.

'What's wrong with your baby?' one of them will ask a friend.

'My baby has a sore tummy,' the friend might answer.

'And what is wrong with your baby?' they ask Rachel or Bethany.

'My baby has meningitis,' she will reply.

This has brought about many strange and disbelieving looks at playgroup as Bethany at three years, barely able to say anything harder than Mummy and Daddy, comes out with 'meningitis'.

We had a few hiccups when we got home, mostly to do with Stephen not liking his medicine. In hospital he had been given his antibiotics through an intravenous line, but now he was taking them by mouth. He had become so used to taking milk in a bottle that he no longer wanted to be breast fed. My own milk supply slowly diminished and no matter how hard I tried to re-establish the breast feeding I soon realised that it wasn't to be. It took a long time for the hair on his head to grow back in where it had been shaved. But apart from that he put on weight as he should and looked no different from any other normal, healthy baby boy. The girls still played up from time to time as any two and four year olds do, but I was rested and more able to cope. That week was a real turning point in our lives. Elgin became home, and we learnt to enjoy it and make new friends. Alistair thrived on his work and life settled down into a more manageable routine.

As I write this account of that very short period in our lives I realise how important and memorable it was, not only for me but for the whole of our family. Parts I have wept over as I have relived the traumas of that time, trying to convey something of what we went through. But I do not resent that interruption in our life. I have never found myself saying. 'Why us?' because throughout it all I was so aware of God. Not that I always understood what he was doing, but I felt sure that in time I would be able to praise him and thank him. What for? I couldn't have told you. But I felt a growing closeness and dependence on him as we walked through the experience together.

About a year after Stephen's illness I paid what I thought was just one of the routine trips to the hospital that would be repeated for many years. While I was there I met the consultant who travelled with us to Aberdeen. He examined Stephen very thoroughly, then said, 'This is what makes my job worthwhile. When

I first saw your son, he was so ill that I didn't think that he would make it. But look at him now. It's nothing short of a miracle. He's so well and has come out of this totally unscathed.'

Stephen was tested for hearing loss. (About one in seven meningitis patients are impaired in some way, hearing loss being the most common after-effect.) They performed an amazing test where sound waves were fired into his ears and the echoes recorded. Stephen lay in my arms quite content to let the nurses carry out their work. This was, after all, nothing compared to what he had been through in the past! When the tests came back they showed no hearing loss whatsoever. He is developing well in every area, and although for the first few months he was a bit slow to do things, he is now a bright and happy wee boy. We thank God daily for the twice given gift of our son's life and his health.

Just a week after we returned home we had a visit from a very dear friend who had moved to Glasgow. He sat listening to our story. As he realised how necessary it was to be aware of the symptoms of meningitis we told him what to look for and what to do if they were present. Little did we know that when he was to return to his mother-in-law's house, where they were staying on holiday, he would find his own son displaying these very symptoms. He quickly phoned the doctor and his son was admitted to hospital. When our friend returned home from the hospital he too felt unwell and within a couple of hours he and his wife realised that it was more than a stress headache. He too was rushed by ambulance into hospital. In all, four of his family were admitted with meningitis, including a newborn baby. Fortunately it was viral meningitis, which is rarely life threatening but nasty all the same. Because of his talk with us that afternoon he knew not to take risks but to seek help immediately.

When you read about the symptoms and listen to other people's stories you feel that it must be a fairly straightforward illness to diagnose. Yet even now, having been through the trauma of it all, I am still not confident that I would spot it another time. Eighteen months after Stephen's illness he became unwell again. He had a high temperature, his eyes were glassy and taking no notice of me. He wouldn't drink or sit up and he developed a small pinprick rash on his body. When I turned the light on he moaned and he didn't want to be cuddled. Alistair was away again and I was very frightened, thinking that history was about to repeat itself. I didn't hesitate to phone my GP and, having explained our previous encounters with meningitis, he was at our house within ten minutes. He examined Stephen and found no sign of neck stiffness which is a crucial symptom. He was very reassuring, explaining that the symptoms pointed to a nonspecific virus, and telling me not to hesitate to contact him again if I was at all worried or if the symptoms progressed. By the next morning Stephen was running about as if nothing had happened.

We all have a part to play in God's plan. At night, when I look in on my children, I often look at their beautiful, peaceful faces and wonder what life has in store for them. I wonder about what jobs they will have, whether they will get married and have children, and I look forward to them following Christ for themselves. But when I look at Stephen there is an added poignancy to my thoughts as I anticipate seeing what part Stephen has to play in God's plan. I found his baptism very precious, as we stood before God promising to bring our son up in the ways of the Lord so entering into a covenant with him to do that. I look forward to seeing how God works out his part in the covenant. How I would like to think that Stephen has been saved to serve.

Going Home

The day has come at last,
We're going home!
My heart pounds violently against my chest.
Smiles greet me at every turn.
'We're so happy for you,'
They say.

This afternoon, we're going home!
At last! I say.
Soon, I'll see my little girls,
And my arms will be full once more
With all that is dear to me.
But why does my heart beat so?

The hour has come at last.
We're going home!
Just one last visit from the doctor,
He shakes my hand
And says encouraging things,
But my heart stops
And misses a beat.

The minute has come, at last.
But I am so scared.
We have no monitors at home,
No nurses in white,
Or doctors on call.
Just me and Alistair.

But a doctor does await our return,
With arms open wide,
To care for our son
and quieten my beating heart,
Not just for this hour, this minute, or day.
But for life and eternity.

Postscript

'I love you, Mummy!' a voice called from behind me. I turned around to see a child camouflaged with mud, half way up a tree. An enormous smile greeted me and as he raised a hand to wave, his balance wavered for just a moment, before managing to catch onto a branch.

It is hard to believe that this three-year-old child, big for his age, so full of fun and life, was just three years ago the tiny little baby who was so close to death. He suffered no lasting effects and apart from a slight developmental slowness in the first few months after his illness, he is now doing everything a three-year-old child should be doing. For many children who have suffered from meningitis, the outcome is so different and we are very grateful that our son recovered. There have been recent reports on the news that a vaccine has been produced that should protect us from contracting this illness. It is quite a thought for parents to present their children for yet another injection, but next to the heartache of meningitis, this has to be a good thing. Meningitis is certainly on the increase and prevention is much better than a cure.

'Catch me, Mum!' he shouted as he launched

himself so trustingly into my arms.

'I love you too, my darling,' I whispered.

'But I love you more than all the sweeties in the world,' he said.

But he will never know how much more than that he is loved. And how can he? He doesn't remember the pain and the tears. One day I will let him read this book and maybe he will realise in some way how precious his life is. And I hope that the girls will too realise that this could have happened to either one of them, and that our feelings of gratitude to God for their lives are just as strong.

As we face yet another move – the Highland Theological College has transferred to its own premises in Dingwall, north of Inverness – the memories of those weeks surrounding our last move through to Elgin are all too real. This time I hope that I have learnt to pace myself better, and learnt that I do not need to be Superwoman. But most of all I hope that I can rest in the knowledge that I have a heavenly Father who is caring for us and is big enough to carry all our cares and burdens.

We are looking forward to the move and to seeing how the next phase of our lives unfolds. And we look forward to watching Stephen and his sisters growing up and seeing what is in store for them.

About Meningitis

What is meningitis?
There are two main forms of meningitis: viral meningitis and bacterial meningitis. Viral meningitis is rarely life threatening, unlike bacterial meningitis which carries 100% mortality rate if it is not treated promptly. Around one in ten patients die even with treatment, and about one in seven who survive suffer from some form of after-effects, the most common of which is hearing loss. But with prompt diagnosis and treatment most people make a full recovery.

Who is most at risk?
Young children and the elderly are most at risk.

At any one time around 52% of the population carry in their throats the virus responsible for meningitis. For most people it is harmless and they are never aware of it. It is still not known why for some people this breaks into the meninges, the layered membranes that surround and protect the brain and the spinal cord.

There are two main forms of bacterial meningitis: meningococcal and pneumococcal.

The names represent the different organisms that cause the meninges to become inflamed.

How is it spread?
The bacteria is spread by close contact with someone who is carrying the bacteria. It is spread between people by coughing, sneezing and kissing. The germs cannot live outside the body for long and so they cannot be picked up from water supplies, swimming pools, buildings or factories.

How is it diagnosed?
Initially a physical examination is carried out. If it reveals no other cause for the fever (ie ear infection, tonsillitis etc.) then a lumbar puncture is done. A needle is inserted into the spine and a small amount of spinal fluid removed. If it is cloudy bacterial meningitis is present. This is the only way a definitive diagnosis can be made.

What is the treatment?
The treatment for bacterial meningitis involves hospitalisation and high doses of intravenous antibiotics. Viral meningitis will in most cases disappear without treatment. A delay in the diagnosis and treatment of bacterial meningitis can result in death, or significant complications such as deafness, memory difficulties or learning disabilities.

Can you catch it more than once?
Yes you can! The body doesn't build up an immunity to the bacteria as it does to chicken pox or measles. But someone who has already had meningitis is not at any higher risk than anyone else.

What are the most common symptoms?
Common symptoms for viral and bacterial meningitis include: high temperature, headache with pain and stiffness in the neck when attempting to put the chin to the chest. Babies may be irritable, eat poorly, and cry when picked up. The skin is often pale and blotchy and they may display a dislike to bright lights. In some cases a rash may develop. Rashes often develop with high temperatures, but this rash can be distinguished from the others by means of a simple test. If you place a clear flat glass over the rash, the rash will not disappear.

I cannot stress enough that parents are the experts in their own child. They more than anyone else know when a child is out of sorts and behaving out of character. If we are worried, we need to seek advice, no matter what time of the day or night. Our children are precious gifts from God. We need to take care of them..

A Gift

A precious gift of priceless worth.
Wrapped up in silk of finest cloth.
Its hue like sunrise bright and clear.
The wakening morn of promise near.
The sapphires sparkle an inward beauty
That tells of treasures stored in plenty.
Those rosebuds placed upon it so
Herald peace and love and joy.
This gift needs not to be unwrapped
But daily it will bloom and grow
Until at last in heaven we'll see
The gift he gave to you and me.

LEARNING ABOUT SERIES

Learning to Cope With Depression
Elaine Brown

Learning to Forgive
(Cathy's Story)
Glenn Myers

Learning About The Old Testament
Alan Harman

Learning About Spirituality
(Jesus Our Joy)
Wallace Benn

Learning About Mission
John Brand

Learning to Resist Temptation
Colin Peckham

Learning About Cults
Bryan Williams